WITHDRAWN

S0-FQY-241

3 1526 04943086 8

WITHDRAWN

UNCOMMON WOMEN

Nick Day

Uncommon Women: Royalty

Copyright © 2017
Published by Scobre Educational
Written by Nick Day

All rights reserved.

Printed in the United States of America.

No part of this book may be reproduced in any manner whatsoever
without written permission, except in the case of brief quotations
embodied in critical articles and reviews.

Scobre Educational
42982 Osgood Road
Fremont, CA 94539

www.scobre.com
info@scobre.com

Scobre Educational publications may be purchased for
educational, business, or sales promotional use.

Cover design by Sara Radka
Layout design by Nikki Ramsay
Edited by Kirsten Rue and Lauren Dupuis-Perez
Copyedited by Malia Green
Images sourced from iStock, Shutterstock, Alamy, and Newscom

ISBN: 978-1-62920-579-3 (hardcover)
ISBN: 978-1-62920-578-6 (eBook)

table of contents

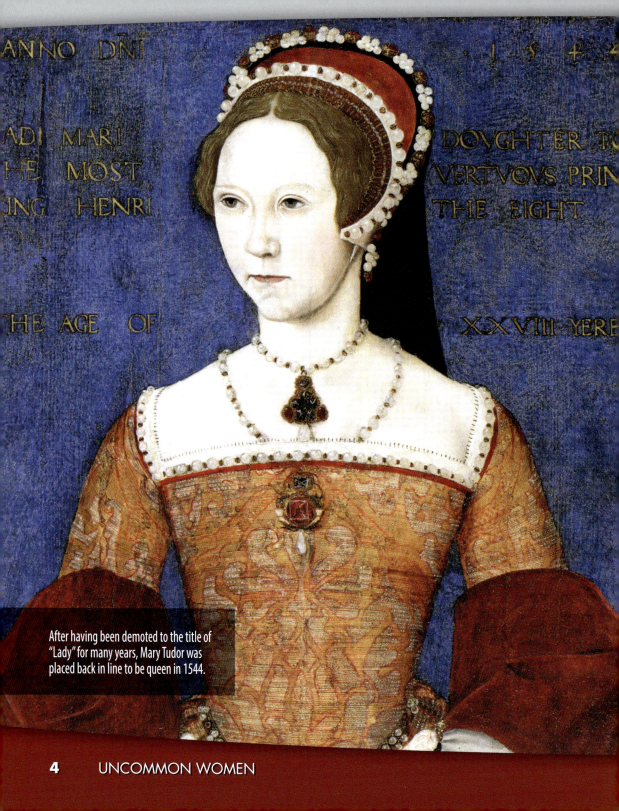

ANNO DŇI   1 5 4 4

ADI MARI   DOVGHTER TO
HE MOST   VERTVOVS PRIN
ING HENRI   THE EIGHT

THE AGE OF   XXVIII YERE

After having been demoted to the title of "Lady" for many years, Mary Tudor was placed back in line to be queen in 1544.

Chapter One
QUEEN MARY, PART I

On a snowy February night in 1516, King Henry VIII and his wife Katherine of Aragon celebrated the birth of their first daughter. It had taken the couple seven long years to finally produce an heir to the throne. The king and queen were happy and relieved—finally, they had a potential an heir. However, Henry still desperately wanted a son.

Little did the king and queen know that their newborn daughter was no ordinary child. Katherine had just given birth to one of the most **notorious**, violent women in the history of England: Mary Tudor, or, as she is better known, Bloody Mary.

From her first breath, Mary played an important role in her father's court. Mary was most valuable to her father as a bargaining chip with other countries. As any king in his era would have done, Henry offered Mary as a potential wife to kings and princes throughout Europe, but especially to his rivals Francis I of France and Charles I of Spain. By offering Mary as a potential wife, Henry hoped to gain power over his international rivals. Love and happiness were not part of the equation.

In March 1522, Charles Poupet de Lachaulx, the imperial ambassador of

DID YOU KNOW?

In 16th century England, educated women were viewed as inferior to other women, since a woman's true job was to be subservient to her husband.

Spain, visited England to meet the young Mary. As soon as Lachaulx entered the royal palace, Mary's mother Katherine insisted that he see Mary dance. Mary, only six years old, had already lost the shyness that most children her age have. She twirled around the room, performing her favorite dance moves with gusto. She was a born performer. Mary also played many songs on the spinet, an early version of the piano. Lachaulx was thrilled.

The meeting between Mary and Lachaulx was a complete success, and Henry arranged a marriage between Mary and Charles, the King of Spain. This was the best outcome Henry and Katherine could have hoped for. Mary spent little time with her new husband-to-be, however, because he was 21 years old. She could not legally live with Charles until she was twelve. Arranging marriages between children, or between children and adults, was a normal practice at this time. Mary had been raised to expect she would be married to another royal family from a faraway country.

Mary's mother Katherine was thrilled because the marriage was another link between her native home of Spain and her new home of England. This, in turn, made Mary more excited about her marriage to Charles. If her mother supported it, then Mary did too. Mary and Katherine were inseparable at the royal palace in England. Mary also took after her mother in her dark looks and her aggressive personality. Their friendship was very strong, but it would be tested when Henry and Katherine's marriage crumbled in the years to come.

Soon after her marriage was arranged, Mary began her education as a royal Spanish lady. Although she was still the sole heir to the English throne, Mary had to prepare to move to Spain before her marriage to Charles. At the same time, Mary knew that if Henry never produced a son to inherit the English throne, she would become Queen of England.

A marriage was arranged between King Charles of Spain and the young Mary. However, the marriage was delayed because Charles was 21 and Mary was only 6.

In the summer of 1527, when Mary was just 11 years old, her parents' marriage began to fall apart. Katherine was becoming too old to have children, and Henry was still desperate to produce a son. Henry began to contemplate divorcing his wife for a younger woman. He already had his eyes on a young **lady-in-waiting**: Anne Boleyn. At this time in England, divorce was not allowed. England was still a Catholic nation, and the Catholic Church did not allow divorce. Henry put his closest advisers to work, trying to find a way around the law, and he was confident they would succeed. Even before it was made official, he told his wife that their marriage was over.

Katherine was crushed, and so was Mary. The process took years, but Henry turned a cold shoulder to his wife and daughter immediately. He said he would never have anything to do with them ever again. Katherine spent her days crying, desperate to change Henry's mind. In one famous moment in 1529, she publicly flung herself at her husband's feet, sobbing and begging him to take her back. He did not.

Five years later, in March 1534, the marriage was over. Henry had inserted himself as the Supreme Head of the Church of England, and separated the Church of England, which was **Protestant**, from the Catholic Church. Though he remained Catholic, he used his position as head of the Church of England to make his own divorce legal. Pope Paul III, the head of the Catholic Church, excommunicated the king. But to Henry, it was worth it—now he could marry Anne Boleyn and finally have a son.

Once the marriage became official, Katherine and

Anne Boleyn was not a member of any royal family before marrying King Henry VIII.

Mary were sent away. Mary's claim to the throne disappeared, as did her arranged marriage to Charles. Henry and Anne's daughter Elizabeth, who would later become Queen Elizabeth I, was now first in line for the throne.

Mary was put under **house arrest** and lived alone in a tower near the royal palace. Katherine was sent far away and almost never saw her daughter. Henry and the English government paid for Katherine and Mary to live while they were banished, since they had no money of their own. They weren't given much, but they did have food and a home, and they were constantly supervised by guards who made sure they didn't try to escape.

Mary was angry with her father, but she was most affected by Henry's new wife, Anne Boleyn. Anne hated Mary and Katherine, and implied that she would like to see them dead. There have been many rumors throughout history

King Henry and Anne Boleyn's relationship was not legal in England—until he removed the Catholic Church from the country, allowing him to marry Anne.

DID YOU KNOW?

The legend of Anne Boleyn lives on, even today. There are endless stories of visitors to the Tower of London, late at night, spotting Anne's ghost roaming the halls, carrying her head under her arm.

that Anne actually poisoned Katherine, but none of them have ever been proven. Katherine lived alone in a deep depression until she died in 1536. Mary was not even permitted to visit her dying mother.

The drama of Henry's time as king did not stop there, however. Later in 1536, Queen Anne and Henry had a falling out. Henry was angry because Anne had also not been able to produce a male heir to his throne. Their marriage in shambles, Henry had Anne executed. The charges that Henry pressed against his wife were **bizarre**, ranging from high **treason** to witchcraft. Henry claimed that Anne was making plans to kill him, so he had her killed. The ugly truth is that Henry would stop at nothing to have a son, so rather than go through another divorce, he invented charges against Anne so he could marry

Anne Boleyn was executed at the Tower of London.

another woman.

With Anne out of the picture, Mary had a new hope of reconnecting with her father. She still did not love him, and had not forgiven him for the way he treated her mother, yet she knew that making Henry happy was her only chance at a better life. She had been under house arrest in a tower for over two years and was desperate to improve her situation.

King Henry VIII was one of the most destructive kings in all of English history.

When Mary asked her father if she could come back to live with him at court, Henry presented her with a choice. She could continue living in the tower, or could sign papers saying that Katherine and Henry's marriage had never been valid, and therefore Mary herself was not heir to the throne. Mary had no choice, and signed the document. She was once again a princess.

Mary Tudor was one of the
most feared Queens of England.

Chapter Two
QUEEN MARY, PART II

For ten more years, Mary lived in the royal palace with her father, his different wives, and her half-siblings. Henry's third wife, Jane Seymour, finally gave birth to a boy, Edward, in 1537. Because he was a boy, Edward was first in line for the throne after his father.

Mary's life at court went back to being fairly simple and calm. She was once again living the life of a princess, though by now she was a 21-year-old woman. Mary was a very different person from the little girl who had danced, played the spinet, and charmed visitors at court. She had become serious and angry after everything that had happened to her and her family. Mary had little to do with

Jane Seymour was another woman from outside of royal circles that King Henry chose to marry. She finally gave King Henry what none of his other wives could: a son.

her father, which was exactly how she wanted it. She wasn't there to be anyone's friend. She was there to claim the crown—her crown, which, she believed, had been unfairly ripped from her hands.

On a blustery January night in 1547, things changed again. Henry VIII,

King Edward was crowned when he was just 10 years old, because he was the oldest male in the line of succession to the throne.

overweight and sickly, died in the royal palace. If Henry and Jane Seymour had not conceived a boy, Mary would have been the new queen. Though she had signed the document nullifying her parents' marriage, Mary still had the best claim to the throne as Henry's oldest child. Mary had to watch as her ten-year-old brother, Edward, was crowned King of England. Mary, who was now over 30, was once again a princess in someone else's court.

During Edward's reign as king, Mary became even more focused on becoming queen. Edward could have given his sister an influential role in his court, but instead he did the opposite. He was as cold to Mary as Henry had been. This was mostly due to the fact that Edward and Mary did not see eye-to-eye on anything, especially religion. Mary had taken after her mother Katherine in her religious views. She was a proud Catholic, and thought that England had started on a path to destruction by separating from the Catholic Church.

DID YOU KNOW?

Though he was young, King Edward was not the youngest to be crowned in English history. That title belongs to King Henry VI, who was only 8 months and 25 days old when he was crowned.

Edward had taken after his father, and believed that England was better off the way it was.

The new king's reign did not last nearly as long as expected. In 1552, when he was only 15 and had only been king for five years, Edward fell sick with **tuberculosis**. Although he knew his time as king was over, Edward took decisive action in his final hours. He knew that his sister, Mary, would return England to a Catholic nation, which he rejected. Because of this, Edward signed papers that would stop Mary and Elizabeth from inheriting the throne. Instead, the throne would go to a cousin of Edward's, the Lady Jane Grey. Mary was absolutely stunned. It was the second time she had had the crown ripped from her hands. There would not be a third.

Lady Jane Grey was proclaimed Queen after the death of King Edward. She was installed as Queen by King Edward to prevent Edward's sister, Mary, from taking the throne.

Mary assembled a large army of English citizens who believed that she was the rightful heir. She gathered men, horses, money, and weapons by riding throughout the English countryside and the towns surrounding London. Though she was no match for the queen's army, Mary's militia (a small unofficial army) was powerful and would not back down. Mary and her militia took over Framlingham Castle outside of London and prepared for battle. On the day Lady Jane Grey was unofficially declared queen, Mary issued a proclamation stating that the new queen was defying Mary, the one true Queen of England. And if Lady Jane Grey did not give up the throne, the proclamation said, there would be violent consequences.

Jane was **deposed** on July 19, 1553, after Mary had convinced both the public and Jane's closest advisors that she, Mary, was the rightful heir. Mary rode into London on horseback on August 3, accompanied by more than 800 cheering supporters. Mary immediately executed many of Jane Grey's advisors, and threw Jane herself into the Tower of London; the following February, Grey was executed after being charged with high treason. After going through the official coronation ceremony, which Jane Grey could not complete, Mary became the first official Queen of England.

DID YOU KNOW?

The Tower of London was built in the year 1066. Since then it has been home to thousands of prisoners, and nearly as many executions—including some that were performed in the early 1900s.

Queen Mary wasted no time on the throne. First, she wanted to destroy the Church of England. Mary's sister Elizabeth, who was also her close adviser, was upset by this. Elizabeth begged the queen to take action on other topics, and to help the country in other ways. England was facing major economic problems at the time, mostly due to the many wars that Henry VIII had started and not finished. But Mary was focused. She would not rest until Catholicism was restored. Mary's refusal of her sister's requests drove them apart. Even though Elizabeth had helped Mary to reclaim the throne, they were immediately separated once Mary became queen.

Sisters Mary and Elizabeth clashed early and often in Mary's reign as Queen. Queen Mary was obsessed with making England a Catholic nation once again, and Elizabeth implored her to consider other more urgent issues.

In her first year as queen, Mary once again made England a Catholic nation. In 1554, she passed the infamous Heresy Acts. "Heresy" is a belief or practice that runs against an official set of laws or beliefs—in this case, Catholic laws. The Acts, which were actually old laws that Mary brought back to life, contained strict penalties for any English citizen who disobeyed Catholic law. The most

DID YOU KNOW?

The Church of England, since its separation from the Catholic Church under Henry VIII, has consistently grown in size. Today it contains more than 26 million members.

serious offense a person could commit under the Heresy Acts was practicing any religion other than Catholicism. This offense was punishable by death.

The Heresy Acts had just the effect Mary wanted. Nearly 800 Protestant citizens fled the country, worried they would be killed. However, there were many citizens who did not leave the country, either because they did not take Mary seriously or because they couldn't leave everything behind. In response, Mary made her power known, putting 238 English citizens to death by burning them at the stake. Most of the people that Queen Mary executed were ministers or pastors in the Church of England, and were leaders in their communities.

Was Mary proud of the violence she had started? She certainly flaunted her actions. The heads of former Protestant

John Bradford, a Protestant preacher, was imprisoned in the Tower of London, and was later burned alive under the Heresy Acts.

men and women, thrust onto spikes, lined the streets of London during her reign. Mary was determined to exercise her power over England and its people, and if she had to violently intimidate her citizens in order to get them to follow her orders, so be it. Mary believed that if she didn't remove the Protestants from England, they would infect more of the population, and England would incur the wrath of God. This is how Mary earned her nickname, Bloody Mary. She was responsible for the death of at least 238 English citizens, all of whom did nothing more than attend a Protestant church.

A portrait of Queen Mary in 1558, just before her death. She married, but never produced her own heir to the throne.

Mary did not accomplish much else as Queen of England. She was focused on making England a Catholic nation once again, which took all her energy and time on the throne. Mary became sick with influenza in the spring of 1558, and died at age 42. Her five-year reign as Queen of England was violent and upsetting, and very few people mourned her death. She did marry, but never had a child. Instead, she passed the crown to her half-sister, Elizabeth.

Elizabeth was queen for 45 years.

Chapter Three
QUEEN ELIZABETH I, PART I

Becoming Queen of England in November 1558 was just one more chapter in the unpredictable life of young Elizabeth Tudor. Elizabeth was born to King Henry VIII and his hated second wife, Anne Boleyn, who was publicly executed when Elizabeth was not even three years old. Living as Henry VIII's daughter was never pleasant or easy. She watched her half-sister Mary become queen, only to witness her order the executions of hundreds of people, and drive hundreds more out of the country. Because of her religious beliefs, Mary might have killed Elizabeth, too. Thankfully, Mary ran out of time.

According to legend, Elizabeth was walking in a country meadow one day when two royal officials approached her. It was a bright fall afternoon, and Elizabeth was enjoying the weather. She noticed the men carrying Queen Mary's signet ring, which was passed down from all former kings and queens of England. Elizabeth knew this meant that her sister the queen was dead. She collapsed, giddy, in the tall grass. "This is the Lord's doing, and it is marvelous in our eyes!" she cried in Latin.

When Elizabeth arrived at her coronation ceremony to be crowned queen, she breathed a sigh of relief. She had waited her turn, always in the background, and now she was being rewarded for it. Though she was raised in such a violent and miserable time, Elizabeth Tudor became a very intelligent and independent young woman.

From a young age, Elizabeth had an impressive ear for languages. She had the same royal governess, Catherine Ashley, for almost thirty years. Elizabeth spent every day with Ashley, from the time she was four years old, until after her thirtieth birthday. Ashley taught her many languages during their time together, including French, Flemish, Italian, and Spanish. Over the course of her life, Elizabeth also learned to speak and write Latin, Welsh, Cornish, and Scottish. In fact, by the time she ended her private studies in 1550, at age 17, she was one of the best-educated women of her generation, especially compared to vast majority of women of her generation, who couldn't read English, let alone anything else.

DID YOU KNOW?

It is now common practice for English queens to become highly educated. That being said, the current Queen, Elizabeth II, speaks only English and French fluently.

Elizabeth's intelligence set her apart from other queens of England. Through her rich education as a young woman, Elizabeth developed a lifelong love of learning. Her sister Mary, for example, never valued learning in the same way. Thanks to her appreciation of knowledge and critical thought, Elizabeth was a more successful queen than her sister had been. Elizabeth was a true politician

The young Elizabeth dedicated all her time to her own education. By the time she was 17, she spoke at least five languages.

who had her eye on everything at all times. She was an expert who knew how to lead, how to compromise, and how to talk to people—in nine different languages.

Another important part of Elizabeth's childhood was her relationship with her family. Henry VIII and Anne Boleyn were no one's idea of good parents. Because Elizabeth was a girl, Henry had little to do with her. He was still desperate to have a son, and just looking at yet another daughter made him furious. Because Anne Boleyn was killed when Elizabeth was still a toddler, she grew up with no mother figure in her life. Elizabeth's close relationships with her governesses and ladies-in-waiting were as close as she would ever get to having a mother. Indeed, there was another member of her family who influenced Elizabeth. This was Elizabeth's guardian,

Elizabeth did not have an easy life growing up in Henry VIII's court. She was without a consistent mother figure, and had no relationship with her father.

Thomas Seymour. When she was a young teenager, Elizabeth lived at Seymour's house in Chelsea, London. Seymour terrified young Elizabeth. He often bullied and teased her, and no one was around to stop him. Until she was a legal adult, Elizabeth was forced to live in this miserable situation. One way Elizabeth dealt with Seymour was by turning to her books. She developed a lifelong habit of waking up extremely early every day to read, hiding in her room from sunup to sundown in order to avoid her guardian's terrors.

Elizabeth was sent away for a time to live with her guardian, Thomas Seymour. He was regularly abusive to Elizabeth, but she was forced to live with him until she reached adulthood.

Elizabeth would never forget Seymour. The most significant effect he had on Elizabeth was that for the remainder of her life, she was never interested in men or marriage. In fact, she became known as the "Virgin Queen." She had male friends, but Elizabeth kept her distance from men throughout her life.

Queen Elizabeth claimed the crown in 1558 in theatrical fashion. The people of England were relieved to see the previous queen gone, and a very different one taking her place.

And though she had many suitors—from France, Spain, Sweden, and the Netherlands, among others—she never accepted any of their offers. Elizabeth

DID YOU KNOW?

Carrying royalty in a "litter," as pictured here, has long been a common practice. Roman royalty was carried in similar fashion thousands of years ago.

remained an independent woman, determined to go through life alone.

This was the woman who claimed the crown in London in 1558, at age 25. She was a warm and welcome presence to the people of England. As she rode toward the royal palace, Elizabeth made quite an impression. She greeted her public with a true smile. She seemed happy to be queen, unlike her sister.

In fact, the citizens of London were so thrilled to see Elizabeth take the throne that the city erupted in celebration. People dragged long wooden tables out of their houses into the street, and London's citizens had a massive public feast in Elizabeth's honor. Bonfires were lit around the city, and the people rejoiced. A new era in history had just begun. Elizabeth would come to not only change the course of English history, but the history of the world as well. It was a time of exploration and creation throughout Europe: the Elizabethan Era.

Queen Elizabeth I was crowned amidst a period of great turmoil in England. She was determined to reform the nation and lift her citizens out of poverty.

Chapter Four
QUEEN ELIZABETH I, PART II

On the day of her coronation, Elizabeth was given a tour of London. She rode into the center of town in a carriage with her longtime friend Robert Dudley. As the country had become poorer and poorer in the previous decades, many English citizens had fled to London and built slums on the streets in which to live. By now, on Elizabeth's coronation day, the slums had expanded greatly, housing thousands of people. Although the citizens of London were overjoyed to welcome their new queen, Elizabeth couldn't help but worry about their quality of life as they cheered her on from their dingy housing.

In a speech on the day of her coronation, Elizabeth vowed to help everyone who was suffering. Standing in front of the royal palace, she gave a famous address about how she would act as queen. She stated that as queen, she represented two beings. Half of her was "the body politic," the English government; the other half of her was "the body natural," an everyday English citizen, just like everyone else. This idea was revolutionary for its time. Elizabeth's predecessors, Henry VIII and Mary especially, did not think of themselves as normal at all. They viewed themselves as something more than human. They thought they were more connected to God than to other people, and they were supposed to watch over their citizens as His agents.

Elizabeth's words shocked people. Never before had a king or queen been so humble. She asked for everyone's help in making England a better place, expressing that she needed everyone to work together to achieve happiness. In the modern world, hearing a politician say things like this is fairly common, but it was completely new in 1558. Elizabeth was inspiring, and inspired the English people to look ahead to a better future.

On top of the poverty that London was suffering, Elizabeth was also faced with England's religious debate. This was the debate that was begun by Elizabeth's father, Henry VIII, when he separated the Church of England from the Catholic Church. It had been continued by Queen Mary, to a bloody end. When Elizabeth became queen, the country was confused. There were both Catholics and Protestants living in England.

Elizabeth knew that if she tried to force the country into agreeing about religion, she would spark violence all over again. Instead, she had a simple response to the problem. Elizabeth told the people that they were first and foremost English citizens. Their religious beliefs were less important than their belief in their country. And for the most part, people listened, as they always did, to Elizabeth.

This was a major piece of Elizabeth's legacy. She was queen at a time when

England's reputation was at an all-time low. Since the country had such a bad economy, other European countries didn't even want to lend it money, as they weren't sure England would ever pay them back. Elizabeth convinced England to believe in itself again.

Early in her reign as queen, Elizabeth was tested when religious fighting in neighboring Scotland bled into England. Elizabeth's cousin Mary was the new Catholic Queen of Scotland (she is commonly referred to as Mary,

Queen Elizabeth's cousin Mary, the Queen of Scotland, was chased out of her country during a period of religious uprising.

Queen of Scots). In 1568, 10 years after Elizabeth had taken the throne, Mary was overthrown by Protestant rebels and imprisoned in Scotland. The rebels claimed that Mary had murdered her husband, but the charges against her were unclear. Scotland was going through the same religious unrest that England was facing, and it had taken its queen fully off the throne. Soon after, Mary arrived in England, seeking Elizabeth's protection. Elizabeth had no choice but to house

Mary in English castles where English guards could protect her.

Elizabeth was faced with a difficult decision. While she wanted to protect her cousin, Elizabeth also knew that helping Mary might be harmful to herself. Mary was Catholic, and if Elizabeth allowed her to stay in England, she might marry a powerful Catholic member of the royal family—and could possibly challenge Elizabeth for the throne. When Elizabeth asked Scotland if she could send Mary back, the new Catholic leadership said that Mary would face certain death if she ever set foot in Scotland again.

What would Elizabeth do? She planned on being queen for decades to come, and had many more things yet to accomplish. She would not let Mary force the crown from her hands. Elizabeth decided to limit Mary's power, and imprisoned her cousin in the castles that were originally for Mary's protection. Mary was regularly moved between Sheffield Castle, Wingfield Manor, and Chatsworth House, which were all far from London, and also far from the sea. Mary could not escape.

DID YOU KNOW?

English royalty often moved between castles and houses all year long. This was because castles became unpleasant to live in after a number of months, and had to be purged of human waste and grime.

Things got even worse in the summer of 1571, when a Catholic rebellion erupted in northern England. As the Protestants took over in Scotland, Catholics were chased out and followed

Queen Elizabeth was threatened by Queen Mary's presence in England, so she had her kept in distant houses around the nation. One of these homes was Chatsworth House, which still stands today.

Mary, their former queen, southward into England. Elizabeth was greatly disturbed by this. She put even more protection on Mary and moved her farther into the countryside. Elizabeth sent troops to **intervene** in the war. They stopped the rebellion in England, and also eased the civil war in Scotland.

Mary was never released. In 1571, Elizabeth had Mary moved to a manor house far from London, which was surrounded by a large moat. Elizabeth was content to leave her cousin in custody until, in 1586, Elizabeth intercepted a letter from Mary that made it clear Mary was organizing an assassination attempt on the queen. Elizabeth was truly hurt. She had shown patience to her cousin, and given her support. In response, Mary had betrayed her.

Days after discovering the assassination plot, Elizabeth ordered the execution of her cousin Mary, Queen of Scots. Though her advisers begged her to organize a full legal trial, Elizabeth would not wait. She wanted to bring Mary to justice herself.

Mary was executed on the morning of February

After learning of her cousin Queen Mary's intent to overthrow her, Queen Elizabeth sentenced Mary to death by execution.

8, 1587. Elizabeth looked on as her cousin was led to the guillotine. After the execution was completed, a strange thing happened: something crawled out of Mary's skirts, which were now lying still on the ground. It was a small terrier—one of Mary's beloved dogs. She had brought the little dog in her pocket to her execution, to comfort her. After the execution was over, the little dog refused to be parted from its owner's body; it yapped frantically, in a tragic display of loyalty. Elizabeth looked on, unmoved.

Mary, Queen of Scots, was executed in 1587. Though her cousin, Queen Elizabeth, would have liked to avoid it, she viewed the execution as a political necessity.

While Elizabeth told the people of England to believe in their country, she also tried to strengthen England's image around the world. A different queen might have backed down in the wars England was always fighting with its neighboring European countries. Elizabeth, on the other hand, was confident, and

Sir Francis Drake is one of the most important explorers in all of English history. Queen Elizabeth was so impressed with Drake's work that she knighted him, the highest honor she could bestow.

continued to press Spain and France. Elizabeth also emphasized the importance of international exploration, and this focus on the exploration of the Western world would result in huge rewards.

In 1570, England had a reason to celebrate. Elizabeth had recently sent the famous explorer Sir Francis Drake out on a mission to survey Spanish territory. In this time, this was how kings and queens tried to conquer new lands: they would send ships out to explore enemy lands and find their weaknesses. If weaknesses were found, the ships would attack. England did not necessarily conquer new land in Spain, but the English did want to provoke Spain to war. If Spain was provoked, England could fight them, and if the English could

DID YOU KNOW?

While Drake was a hero to the English, the Spanish viewed him as a pirate. King Philip II of Spain put a bounty of 40,000 ducats on Drake's head.

won, they could come away with money, ships, and weapons.

This is exactly what Sir Francis Drake and his men did. When Drake's ship arrived in Cadiz, a port city in southwestern Spain, they noticed a large ship sitting unattended at a dock. When they got closer, they found that the ship was carrying exotic fur, gold, and other merchandise worth more than 40,000 ducats (more than $3.5 million today). Drake and his men raided the ship, stole everything, and sailed back to England. This solved two of England's problems in one fell swoop: the country was 40,000 ducats richer, and they had successfully provoked Spain into battle.

The plan worked. The Spanish were completely surprised, and immediately planned an attack. The Spanish Emperor unleashed the Armada, a huge fleet of over forty ships, which sailed toward England. Spain was not used to being embarrassed on such a large scale, and they wanted revenge.

On July 29, 1588, the Armada arrived in the English Channel, and was easily defeated. The English warships scattered the ships of the Armada and chased them out of English waters. The victory was a great cause for celebration across England, and Elizabeth was ecstatic. She issued a famous speech after the victory, yelling, "I know I have the body but of a weak and feeble woman, but I have the heart and stomach of a king, and of a King of England too, and think foul scorn that Parma or Spain, or any Prince of Europe should dare to invade the borders of my realm!" The English people were overjoyed, and praised their queen. Elizabeth had done two things at once in her victory over the Armada. She had provided the English economy with the money it so desperately needed, and had helped to improve England's image worldwide. All of a sudden, England was a world power that needed to be feared.

This was England's second major international victory during Elizabeth's reign. The first occurred in 1586, when England's first territory in North America was created. Sir Walter Raleigh, an English explorer, had already conducted three

English warships took up arms against a fleet of Spanish invaders, and easily won. This international victory was a point of pride for Queen Elizabeth, who looked to strengthen England's international image.

exploration of North America. Yet Elizabeth was skeptical of Raleigh's intentions until 1586, when Raleigh and his men took control of a territory and called it "Virginia," in honor of Elizabeth, "The Virgin Queen." Elizabeth was thrilled.

Even in Elizabeth's time, England's exploration of North America was considered a significant achievement. Of course, not even Elizabeth could guess how much England would one day control, and how much they would one day lose. Elizabeth had already followed through on her promises of improving England's status as a nation. Unlike the time during the reigns of her father Henry VIII, her brother Edward, or her sister Mary, England now had a strong international reputation. Elizabeth was taking England into the future she had always promised.

The first half of Elizabeth's time as Queen of England was a good time to be an English citizen. But in Elizabeth's later years, things in England began to sour.

Sir Walter Raleigh is another important English explorer. He provided Queen Elizabeth with England's first territory in North America, which he called "Virginia," in honor of Elizabeth, "The Virgin Queen."

Though she oversaw the victory against the Spanish Armada in 1588, Queen Elizabeth did not have success in her larger war with Spain. At the same time, England was at war with Ireland, which dragged on with no end in sight. While Elizabeth told the English people that they would win someday, she was not able to shine a positive light on the main problem of the war: England's loss of money. England had sunk too much money into paying for its armies and navies, and the wars were showing no signs of stopping.

Eventually, the wars abated, and England returned to relative peace. It was not a perfect time, however, because the nation still sorely lacked the money it had sunk into years of international conflict. During this lull, England was somewhat revived from within, from its people, as English culture blossomed.

William Shakespeare was a prominent example of this cultural awakening. Although he was already established as a leading figure in English culture, Shakespeare became much more successful, writing his great plays during the second half of Elizabeth's reign. Artists across England were inspired to create plays, poetry, paintings, sculptures, music, dance, and architecture. Led by Shakespeare and another famous playwright, Christopher Marlowe, the English theatre became particularly successful.

Other forms of art also flourished in Elizabethan England. The visual arts, especially painting, went through major changes during Elizabeth's time. The art

DID YOU KNOW?

1589 saw the production of Shakespeare's first play, *King Henry VI*, which he wrote at just 25 years of age.

of portraiture became highly developed, as Elizabethan Era painters devoted a large amount of effort to small details in their work, focusing on capturing every single part of their subject. Queen Elizabeth herself often had her portrait painted, but restricted her painters from doing too-lifelike a portrait of her. Especially in her later years, Elizabeth was very concerned with her image, and did not let her painters portray her wrinkles or her infamous black teeth.

The art of architecture also flourished in Elizabethan England. It became popular in this time for the upper classes to build large estates in the countryside of England, far from the city. These estates, manicured perfectly over the centuries, still exist today and remain in possession of certain families. There were no professional architects in Elizabethan England, but as the art of building a beautiful and unique home became popular, so did the profession of architecture.

The Elizabethan Age is now regarded as a major turning point in English cultural history. Elizabeth herself was a strong supporter of the arts. Though it was not traditional for a queen to sit in the audience at public performances, Elizabeth attended the first performance of *A Midsummer Night's Dream* in 1595, and was greatly pleased.

This was how Elizabeth spent the last decade of her time as queen. The English people still respected her, though they were ready for a new sense of energy and purpose in their leader. Elizabeth had led England through many major wars, severe economic depression—and had even thwarted an assassination attempt. However, her time on the throne was coming to an end.

In the fall of 1602, when Elizabeth was almost 70 years old, many of her close friends had passed away from sickness. Elizabeth was truly lonely, and became deeply depressed. She had been queen much longer than others had, and she was tired. In late March of 1603, the queen died from symptoms of pneumonia; her exhausted immune system could not withstand the sickness.

One problem Elizabeth had to face during her final weeks as queen was naming an heir. Because she never married, she never had any children. This left

Queen Elizabeth I is still viewed as one of the most influential leaders in all of English history. England saw incredible progress during her 45-year reign.

King James of Scotland was hand-picked by Queen Elizabeth to be her replacement. Because she had no husband and no children, Elizabeth could choose the replacement she thought would be most successful.

her with an opportunity to choose the most deserving replacement. She chose James VI of Scotland to be the next king. She had known James quite well during

DID YOU KNOW?

Late in life, Queen Elizabeth lost all of her hair and teeth, and ordered all mirrors taken out of her castle so she could avoid seeing her reflection.

her last decade as queen, and she respected him. After all, James had played a major role in soothing the civil wars in Scotland that Elizabeth could not solve alone. She knew he would be a worthy replacement as King of England.

Elizabeth's time as Queen of England was complicated, and many people have different opinions about what kind of queen she really was. While she remained famous after her death for the tough stance she took toward other countries—such as her attack on Spain—others pointed out that she cost England a great deal financially. While she was kinder to the English people than her father Henry and her sister Mary, Elizabeth did not quite bring England together the way she said she would.

Elizabeth is remembered as a unique figure in the history of England, and in the history of the world. There have been few monarchs with such a deep passion for leadership and undying love for their people. And even rarer than this kind of monarch, is this kind of queen. Elizabeth achieved great things, and changed the history of the world, without anyone else holding her hand.

GLOSSARY

bizarre: strange, odd

deposed: removed someone from rule by force

house arrest: being imprisoned in one's own house instead of in jail

intervene: to try and prevent something from happening

lady-in-waiting: a female attendant to a queen, princess, or noblewoman who is usually of noble birth herself

notorious: to be famous or well-known, usually for something bad

Protestant: a follower of the Protestant faith, a type of Christianity

treason: the crime of betraying one's country

tuberculosis: a bad and often deadly disease of the lungs

BIBLIOGRAPHY

Erickson, Carolly. Bloody Mary. New York: St. Martin's Griffin, 1978.

Edwards, John. Mary I: England's Catholic Queen. New Haven, CT: Yale University Press, 2011.

Ronald, Susan. The Pirate Queen: Queen Elizabeth I, Her Pirate Adventures, and the Dawn of an Empire. New York: Harper Collins, 2007.

Whitelock, Anna. Mary Tudor: Princess, Bastard, Queen. New York: Random House, 2009.

http://englishhistory.net/tudor/monarchs/eliz5.html